Jerky
Cookbook

Ultimate Cookbook for Making Dried Beef, Fish, Poultry, Game, and Etc. Recipes

By Adam Jones

TABLE OF CONTENTS

INTRODUCTION

To most of the meat "Jerky" aficionados out there in the whole wide world, the process of drying a meat and making a Jerky out of it is nothing short of a form of art, or even a hobby. There is something very calm and relaxing yet extremely satisfying to see your favorite slice of meat turn into a tenderly chewable piece of edible that is packed to the brim with flavors. If you are new to this field, then you must first learn to appreciate the basics of the process if you hope to achieve mastery over it. Therefore, I have dedicated the first few chapters of this book to give you a good idea of the process of drying your meat and preparing a jerky in order to ensure that you have a firm understanding of it. I shall be breaking everything down into tiny bite-sized portions for you to easily digest and understand.

CHAPTER-1 BEEF

PINEAPPLE FLAVORED SRIRACHA SMOKED BEEF JERKY

(COOKING TIME 5 HOURS 10 MINUTES)

INGREDIENTS FOR **10** SERVINGS

- Top Round Lean Beef (2.5-lb., 2.3-kg.)

THE MARINADE

- Soy sauce – 2 ½ cups
- Brown sugar – ¾ cup
- Ground ginger – ½ teaspoon
- Pineapple juice – 1 ½ cups
- Sriracha sauce – 3 tablespoons
- Ground chili – ½ teaspoon
- Hoisin sauce – 3 tablespoons
- Onion powder – 1 tablespoon
- Rice wine vinegar – 3 tablespoons
- Minced garlic – 3 tablespoons

THE HEAT

- Hickory wood pellets

METHOD

1. Cut the lean beef against the grain into ¼-inch slices then set aside.
2. Pour soy sauce, pineapple juice, sriracha sauce, and hoisin sauce to a zipper-lock plastic bag then season with brown sugar, ground ginger, ground chili, onion powder, red wine vinegar, and minced garlic. Mix well.
3. Add the jerky to the plastic bag then shake to coat.
4. Marinade the jerky for at least 6 hours or overnight and store in the fridge to keep it fresh.
5. On the next day, take the marinated jerky out of the fridge and thaw at room temperature.
6. Next, plug the wood pellet smoker then fill the hopper with the wood pellet. Turn the wood pellet smoker on and set the temperature to 165°F (74°C).
7. Wait until the wood pellet smoker is ready then arrange the marinated jerky in the smoker. Give space between the jerky.
8. Smoke the jerky for 5 hours and turning them once every 2 hours.
9. Once it is done, take the smoked jerky out of the wood pellet smoker and let it cool for approximately 30 minutes.
10. Serve and enjoy.

SMOKED SIRLOIN JERKY BLACK PEPPER

(COOKING TIME 7 HOURS 10 MINUTES)

INGREDIENTS FOR 10 SERVINGS

- Sirloin Tip Beef (3-lb., 1.4-kg.)

THE MARINADE

- Ground black pepper – 2 tablespoons

- Soy sauce – 2 cups

- Cider vinegar – 2 tablespoons

- Worcestershire sauce – 1 tablespoon

- Hot sauce – 1 teaspoon

14

THE HEAT

- Hickory wood pellets

METHOD

1. Cut the lean beef against the grain into ½ inch slices then set aside.

2. Combine soy sauce with black pepper, cider vinegar, Worcestershire sauce, and hot sauce then mix well.

3. Add the jerky to the spice mixture then marinate overnight. Store in the fridge to keep the jerky fresh.

4. On the next day, take the marinated jerky out of the fridge and thaw at room temperature.

5. Next, plug the wood pellet smoker then fill the hopper with the wood pellet. Turn the wood pellet smoker on and set the temperature to 160°F (71°C).

6. Arrange the seasoned jerky in the wood pellet smoker and give space between each sliced beef.

7. Smoke the jerky for 7 hours or until the edges of the smoked beef jerky appear dry.

8. Once it is done, remove the smoked jerky from the wood pellet smoker and serve.

9. Enjoy!

SPICY SMOKED BEEF JERKY WITH TERIYAKI SEASONING

(COOKING TIME 5 HOURS 10 MINUTES)

Ingredients for 10 servings

- Eye of Round Beef (3-lb., 1.4-kg.)

The Marinade

- Grated garlic – 2 teaspoons
- Grated ginger – ½ teaspoon
- Vegetable oil – 3 tablespoons
- Sesame oil – 1 tablespoon
- Japanese rice wine – 2 cups
- Honey – 1 cup
- Brown sugar – 1 cup
- Rice vinegar – ¼ cup
- Red chili flakes – 1 teaspoon

The Spray

- Apple juice – ½ cup

The Heat

- Pecan wood pellets

METHOD

1. Cut the lean beef into ¼-inch then set aside.

2. Combine grated garlic with grated ginger, brown sugar, and red chili flakes then mix well.

3. Pour vegetable oil, sesame oil, Japanese rice wine, honey, and rice vinegar over the spices then stir until incorporated.

4. Submerge the jerky in the spice mixture then marinate for at least 8 hours or overnight. Store in the fridge to keep the jerky fresh.

5. On the next day, remove the marinated jerky from the fridge and thaw at room temperature.

6. Next, plug the wood pellet smoker then fill the hopper with the wood pellet. Turn the wood pellet smoker on and set the temperature to 165°F (74°C).

7. Arrange the seasoned jerky on the grill and smoke for 5 hours.

8. Flip the jerky once every hour and spray apple juice over the jerky whenever you think that the jerky is dehydrating too fast.

9. Once it is done, remove the smoked beef jerky from the wood pellet smoker and transfer it to a serving dish. Let it cool.

10. Serve and enjoy.

No Sugar Smoked Beef Jerky Garlic

(Cooking Time 6 Hours 10 Minutes)

Ingredients for 10 servings

- Flank steak (4-lbs., 1.8-kg.)

THE RUB

- Salt – 3 tablespoons
- Black pepper – 1 ½ teaspoons
- Garlic powder – ¼ cup
- Chili powder – 1 tablespoon

THE HEAT

- Mesquite wood pellets

METHOD

1. Trim the excess fat from the flank steak then cut the meat into ⅛- inch thin slices against the grain. Set aside.

2. Place salt, black pepper, garlic powder, and chili powder in a bowl then mix well.

3. Rub the jerky with the spice mixture then let it rest for 2 hours. Store in the fridge to keep it fresh.

4. Next, plug the wood pellet smoker then fill the hopper with the wood pellet. Turn the wood pellet smoker on and set the temperature to 165°F (74°C).

5. Place the seasoned jerky in the wood pellet smoker and smoke for 6 hours. Flip the jerky after 3 hours of smoking.

6. Once the jerky is done, remove it from the wood pellet smoker and transfer it to a serving dish.

7. Let it cool and serve.

8. Enjoy!

Smoked Beef Jerky with Sweet Maple Marinade

(Cooking Time 5 Hours 10 Minutes)

Ingredients for 10 servings

- Bottom Round Lean Beef (2.5-lb., 2.3-kg.)

The Marinade

- Maple syrup – ¼ cup
- Molasses – 2 tablespoons
- White sugar – ¼ cup
- Liquid smoke – 2 tablespoons
- Salt – ½ teaspoon
- Pepper – ¼ teaspoon
- Cold water – ¼ cup

THE HEAT

- Cherry wood pellets

METHOD

1. Cut the beef into ⅛-inch slices then place in a zipper-lock plastic bag.

2. In a bowl, combine maple syrup with molasses, white sugar, liquid smoke, salt, pepper, and cold water then stir until mixed.

3. Pour the spice mixture into the zipper-lock plastic bag then seal it properly.

4. Shake the plastic bag until the jerky is completely coated with spice mixture then marinate for overnight. Store in the fridge to keep it fresh.

5. On the next day, remove the seasoned jerky from the fridge and thaw at room temperature.

6. Next, plug the wood pellet smoker then fill the hopper with the wood pellet. Turn the wood pellet smoker on and set the temperature to 160°F (71°C).

7. Prick each seasoned jerky with a toothpick then hang it on the grill. Repeat with the remaining seasoned jerky.

8. Smoke the jerky for 5 hours and once it is done, remove from the wood pellet smoker.

9. Let the smoked jerky cool and discard the toothpicks.

10. Place the smoked jerky on a serving dish then serve.

11. Enjoy!

Sweet Bourbon Smoked Beef Jerky

(Cooking Time 6 Hours 10 Minutes)

Ingredients for 10 servings

- Top Round Lean Beef (3-lb., 1.4-kg.)

The Marinade

- Bourbon – ¾ cup
- Liquid smoke – 1 tablespoon
- Salt – ¼ teaspoon
- Molasses – 1 tablespoon
- Brown sugar – ¼ cup
- Black pepper – 2 teaspoons
- Soy sauce – ¼ cup
- Worcestershire sauce – ¼ cup

The Heat

- Hickory wood pellets

Method

1. Trim the fat from the beef then place it in the freezer for an hour.

2. In the meantime, combine bourbon with liquid smoke, salt, molasses, brown sugar, black pepper, soy sauce, and Worcestershire sauce in a bowl. Stir until incorporated.

3. After an hour, take the beef out of the freezer then cut into ¼-inch slices.

4. Place the jerky in a zipper-lock plastic bag then drizzle the marinade mixture over the jerky.

5. Seal the plastic bag and shake until the jerky is completely seasoned.

6. Marinate the jerky for at least 8 hours or overnight and store in the fridge to keep it fresh.

7. On the next day, take the marinated jerky out of the fridge and thaw at room temperature.

8. Next, plug the wood pellet smoker then fill the hopper with the wood pellet. Turn the wood pellet smoker on and set the temperature to 160°F (71°C).

9. Place the jerky in the wood pellet smoker and smoke it for 6 hours.

10. Check the smoked jerky and once it is done, remove it from the wood pellet smoker.

11. Arrange the smoked jerky in a serving dish then serve.

12. Enjoy!

Gingery Chili Smoked Ground Beef Jerky

(Cooking Time 6 Hours 10 Minutes)

Ingredients for 10 servings

- Ground beef (3-lb., 1.4-kg.)

THE SPICES

- Salt – 1 teaspoon

- Chili powder – 1 tablespoon

- Garlic powder – 1 tablespoon

- Ground ginger – ¾ teaspoon

- Black pepper – ½ teaspoon

- Cayenne pepper – ¼ teaspoon

THE HEAT

- Mesquite wood pellets

METHOD

1. Season the ground beef with salt, chili powder, garlic powder, ground ginger, black pepper, and cayenne pepper. Mix until combined.

2. Refrigerate the seasoned ground beef for at least 4 hours or more, and then transfer it to a jerky gun.

3. Shoot a strip of jerky on a dehydrator tray then repeat with the remaining seasoned ground beef.

4. Next, plug the wood pellet smoker then fill the hopper with the wood pellet. Turn the wood pellet smoker on and set the temperature to 165°F (74°C).

5. Smoke the ground beef jerky for 6 hours but check the doneness once every 2 hours.

6. Once it is done, remove the smoked ground beef jerky from the wood pellet smoker and transfer it to a serving dish. Serve and enjoy.

ORANGE AROMA SMOKED BEEF JERKY

(Cooking Time 6 Hours 10 Minutes)

Ingredients for 10 servings

- Top Round Lean Beef (3.5-lb., 2.3-kg.)

The Marinade

- Orange juice – 2 cups

- White vinegar – 3 tablespoons

- Allspice seasoning – 1 tablespoon

- Marjoram – 2 teaspoons

- Salt – ¼ teaspoon

The Heat

- Apple wood pellets

METHOD

1. Cut the beef into ¼-inch slices then place in a zipper-lock plastic bag.

2. Pour orange juice into a bowl then season white vinegar, allspice, marjoram, and salt. Stir until incorporated.

3. Transfer the orange juice mixture to the plastic bag and make sure that the jerky is completely submerged.

4. Marinate the jerky for 8 hours to 24 hours and store it in the fridge to keep it fresh.

5. Take the marinated jerky out of the fridge then discard the liquid. Thaw the jerky at room temperature.

6. Next, plug the wood pellet smoker then fill the hopper with the wood pellet. Turn the wood pellet smoker on and set the temperature to 160°F (71°C).

7. Using skewers prick the jerky and hang in between the wood pellet smoker grate.

8. Smoke the jerky for 5 to 6 hours or until it cracks but not breaks into halves.

9. Remove the smoked jerky from the wood pellet smoker and transfer it to a serving dish.

10. Serve and enjoy.

BEER MARINADE SMOKED BEEF JERKY

(Cooking Time 5 Hours 10 Minutes)

Ingredients for 10 servings

- Sirloin tip (3-lb., 1.4-kg.)

The Marinade

- Beer – 4 cups
- Apple cider vinegar – ½ cup
- Salt – 1 teaspoon
- Brown sugar – ½ cup
- Molasses – 3 tablespoons
- Black pepper – 2 teaspoons
- Garlic powder – 1 tablespoon
- Onion powder – 1 tablespoon

The Heat

- Hickory wood pellets

METHOD

1. Cut the sirloin tip into ⅛-inch slices then place them in a container.

2. Add apple cider vinegar, salt, brown sugar, molasses, black pepper, and onion powder to the beer then stir until incorporated.

3. Pour the beer mixture over the jerky and make sure that the jerky is completely soaked in the liquid mixture.

4. Marinate the jerky overnight and store it in the fridge to keep it fresh.

5. On the next day, take the jerky out of the fridge and strain the marinade.

6. Next, plug the wood pellet smoker then fill the hopper with the wood pellet. Turn the wood pellet smoker on and set the temperature to 165°F (74°C).

7. Using skewers prick the jerky and hang in between the wood pellet smoker grate. Smoke the jerky for 5 hours.

8. Once it is done, remove the smoked beef jerky from the wood pellet smoker and arrange it on a serving dish.

9. Serve and enjoy.

BLACK COFFEE SMOKED BEEF JERKY

(Cooking Time 6 Hours 10 Minutes)

- Flank steak (3-lb., 1.4-kg.)

The Marinade

- Brewed coffee – 1 ½ cups

- Soy sauce – ¾ cup

- Brown sugar – ½ cup

- Worcestershire sauce – ¼ cup

- Molasses – 3 tablespoons

- Cayenne pepper – 1 tablespoon

- Black pepper – 1 tablespoon

The Heat

- Mesquite wood pellets

METHOD

1. Trim the excess fat from the flank steak and cut into ¼-inch slices. Place the jerky in a container.

2. Combine brewed coffee with soy sauce, brown sugar, Worcestershire sauce, molasses, cayenne pepper, and black pepper then stir until well mixed.

3. Pour the coffee mixture over the jerky then stir a bit. Make sure that the jerky is completely soaked in the coffee mixture.

4. Marinate the jerky for at least 6 hours or overnight and store in the fridge to keep it fresh.

5. On the next day, remove the jerky and take it out of the marinade. Discard the excess liquid.

6. Next, plug the wood pellet smoker then fill the hopper with the wood pellet. Turn the wood pellet smoker on and set the temperature to 165°F (74°C).

7. Using skewers prick the jerky and hang in between the wood pellet smoker grate. Smoke the jerky for 6 hours.

8. Once it is done, remove the smoked jerky from the wood pellet smoker and arrange it on a serving dish.

9. Serve and enjoy.

CHAPTER-2 TURKEY AND CHICKEN

SOY SAUCE SMOKED TURKEY JERKY BARBECUE

(COOKING TIME 5 HOURS 10 MINUTES)

INGREDIENTS FOR 10 SERVINGS

- Turkey breast (2.5-lb., 2.3-kg.)

THE MARINADE

- Worcestershire sauce – 2 cups

- Soy sauce – 1 cup

- Liquid smoke – ¼ cup

- Onion powder – 2 tablespoons

- Apple cider vinegar – ¾ cup

- Granulated sugar – 3 tablespoons

- Ketchup – 3 tablespoons

- Honey – 2 tablespoons

- Salt – ¼ teaspoon

- Black pepper – ½ teaspoon

THE HEAT

- Apple wood pellets

METHOD

1. Cut the turkey breast into ¼-inch slices then place it in a container.

2. Mix Worcestershire sauce with soy sauce, liquid smoke, onion powder, apple cider vinegar, granulated sugar, ketchup, honey, salt, and pepper. Stir until incorporated.

3. Pour the spice mixture over the turkey jerky then squeeze a bit until the turkey is completely coated with the spice mixture.

4. Marinate the jerky for 8 hours or overnight and store it in the fridge to keep it fresh.

5. On the next day, remove the seasoned turkey jerky from the fridge and discard the marinade. Thaw the seasoned turkey jerky at room temperature.

6. Next, plug the wood pellet smoker then fill the hopper with the wood pellet. Turn the wood pellet smoker on and set the temperature to 170°F (77°C).

7. Arrange the jerky directly on the wood pellet smoker grates and smoke the jerky for 5 hours.

8. Once it is done, remove the smoked turkey jerky from the wood pellet smoker and transfer it to a serving dish.

9. Serve and enjoy.

Gingery Smoked Turkey Jerky with Sesame Aroma

(Cooking Time 5 Hours 10 Minutes)

INGREDIENTS FOR 10 SERVINGS

- Turkey breast (3-lb., 1.4-kg.)

THE MARINADE

- Soy sauce – 1 cup

- Brown sugar – ½ cup

- Ground ginger – ½ teaspoon

- Worcestershire sauce – 3 tablespoons

- Garlic powder – 1 tablespoon

- Liquid smoke – ¼ teaspoon

- Sesame oil – 2 tablespoons

- Honey – 1 ½ tablespoons

- Black pepper – ½ teaspoon

THE HEAT

- Apple wood pellets

METHOD

1. Combine soy sauce with brown sugar, Worcestershire sauce, ground ginger, garlic powder, liquid smoke, sesame oil, honey, and black pepper then stir well. Set aside.

2. Cut the turkey breast into ¼-inch slices then rub with the spice mixture.

3. Transfer the seasoned jerky to a zipper-lock plastic bag then store it in the fridge to keep it fresh. Marinate the turkey jerky for at least 8 hours or overnight.

4. On the next day, remove the plastic bag with seasoned turkey jerky from the fridge and thaw at room temperature. Discard the excess marinade.

5. Next, plug the wood pellet smoker then fill the hopper with the wood pellet. Turn the wood pellet smoker on and set the temperature to 170°F (77°C).

6. Arrange the turkey jerky on the wood pellet smoker grates and smoke for 5 hours. The smoked turkey jerky will be cracks but not breaks into two pieces or more.

7. Once it is done, remove the smoked turkey jerky from the wood pellet smoker and transfer it to a serving dish.

8. Serve and enjoy.

Maple Glazed Wet Smoked Turkey Jerky

(Cooking Time 5 Hours 30 Minutes)

Ingredients for 10 servings

- Turkey breast (3-lb., 1.4-kg.)

THE MARINADE

- Brown sugar – ¾ cup
- Salt – 1 teaspoon
- Garlic powder – 1 tablespoon

THE GLAZE

- Soy sauce – 3 tablespoons
- Brown sugar – ¼ cup
- Lemon juice – 2 tablespoons
- Maple syrup – ¼ cup
- Black pepper – ¼ teaspoon

THE HEAT

- Apple wood pellets

METHOD

1. Cut the turkey breast into ¼-inch slices then set aside.

2. Combine brown sugar, salt, and garlic powder then mix well.

3. Rub the spice mixture over the jerky and marinate it for at least 8 hours or overnight. Store in the fridge to keep it fresh.

4. On the next day, remove the seasoned jerky from the fridge and thaw at room temperature.

5. Next, plug the wood pellet smoker then fill the hopper with the wood pellet. Turn on the wood pellet smoker and set the temperature to 140°F (60°C).

6. Arrange the seasoned jerky in the wood pellet smoker and smoke for 2 hours and a half.

7. In the meantime, combine soy glaze with brown sugar, lemon juice, maple syrup, and black pepper then stir until incorporated. Set aside.

8. After 2 hours and a half of smoking, increase the temperature of the wood pellet smoker to 170°F (77°C).

9. Baste the glaze mixture over the jerky then continue smoking for another 3 hours. Flip and glaze the smoked jerky once every hour.

10. Once it is done, remove the smoked jerky from the wood pellet smoker and transfer it to a serving dish.

11. Serve and enjoy.

TROPICAL SPICY SMOKED TURKEY JERKY

(Cooking Time 5 Hours 10 Minutes)

Ingredients for 10 servings

- Turkey breast (2.5-lb., 2.3-kg.)

The Marinade

- Pineapple juice – ¾ cup
- Soy sauce – ¾ cup
- Worcestershire sauce – 2 tablespoons
- Black pepper – 1 teaspoon
- Garlic powder – 2 teaspoons
- Chili powder – 1 teaspoon
- Honey – 1 tablespoon

The Heat

- Cherry wood pellets

METHOD

1. Cut the turkey breast into ⅛-inch slices then set aside.

2. Pour pineapple juice into a container then add soy sauce, Worcestershire sauce, and honey to the container.

3. Season the mixture with black pepper, garlic powder, and chili powder then stir until incorporated.

4. Add the turkey jerky to the container then stir a bit until the jerky is completely coated with the spice mixture.

5. Marinate the turkey jerky for at least 8 hours or overnight and store in the fridge to keep it fresh.

6. On the next day, remove the marinated jerky from the fridge and thaw at room temperature.

7. Next, plug the wood pellet smoker then fill the hopper with the wood pellet. Turn the wood pellet smoker on and set the temperature to 165°F (74°C).

8. Using skewers prick the turkey jerky and place in between the wood pellet smoker grates.

9. Smoke the turkey jerky for 5 hours and once it is done, remove from the wood pellet smoker.

10. Place the smoked turkey on a serving dish then serve.

11. Enjoy!

Lemon Ginger Smoked Chicken Jerky

(Cooking Time 6 Hours 10 Minutes)

INGREDIENTS FOR 10 SERVINGS

- Chicken breast (5-lb., 2.3-kg.)

THE MARINADE

- Lemon juice – ¼ cup
- Ground ginger – 1 teaspoon
- Ground turmeric – ½ teaspoon
- Minced garlic – 2 tablespoons
- Cumin – 2 tablespoons
- Smoked paprika – 2 tablespoons
- Oregano – 2 teaspoons
- Apple cider vinegar – 2 tablespoons
- Olive oil – 2 tablespoons
- Soy sauce – 3 tablespoons
- Salt – 1 teaspoon

THE HEAT

- Hickory wood pellets

METHOD

1. Trim the excess fat of the chicken breast then cut it into ¼-inch slices. Set aside.

2. Combine the marinade ingredients—lemon juice, ground ginger, turmeric, minced garlic, cumin, smoked paprika, oregano, apple cider vinegar, olive oil, soy sauce, and salt. Mix well.

3. Rub the chicken jerky with the spice mixture then marinade overnight. Store the marinated chicken jerky in the fridge to keep it fresh.

4. On the next day, remove the marinated chicken jerky from the fridge and thaw at room temperature.

5. Transfer the marinated chicken jerky to a colander and gently discard the excess liquid. Do not rinse.

6. Next, plug the wood pellet smoker then fill the hopper with the wood pellet. Turn the wood pellet smoker on and set the temperature to 160°F (71°C).

7. Smoke the chicken jerky for 3 hours then increase the temperature of the wood pellet smoker to 185°F (85°C).

8. Continue smoking the chicken jerky for another 3 hours or until it cracks but not breaks into halves.

9. Once it is done, remove the smoked chicken jerky from the wood pellet smoker and place it on a serving dish.

10. Serve and enjoy.

Spicy Smoked Chicken Jerky Garlic

(Cooking Time 5 Hours 10 Minutes)

Ingredients for 10 servings

- Chicken breast (4-lbs., 1.8-kg.)

The Marinade

- Garlic powder – 2 tablespoons
- Onion powder – 1 tablespoon
- White pepper – ¼ teaspoon
- Black pepper – ¼ teaspoon
- Cayenne pepper – 2 tablespoons
- Red chili flakes – 2 tablespoons
- Salt – ¾ teaspoon

THE HEAT

- Mesquite wood pellets

METHOD

1. Discard the excess fat of the chicken breast then cut it into ¼-inch slices.

2. Sprinkle garlic powder, onion powder, white pepper, black pepper, cayenne pepper, red chili flakes, and salt over the chicken then squeeze until the chicken jerky is completely coated with the spice mixture.

3. Marinate the chicken jerky for at least 8 hours or overnight and store in the fridge to keep it fresh.

4. On the next day, take the marinated chicken out of the fridge and thaw at room temperature.

5. Next, plug the wood pellet smoker then fill the hopper with the wood pellet. Turn the wood pellet smoker on and set the temperature to 165°F (74°C).

6. Smoke the chicken jerky for 5 hours or until it cracks then remove from the wood pellet smoker.

7. Place the smoked chicken jerky on a serving dish then enjoy!

Honey Glazed Smoked Chicken Jerky Rosemary

(Cooking Time 6 Hours 10 Minutes)

Ingredients for 10 servings

- Chicken breast (5-lb., 2.3-kg.)

The Marinade

- Chopped fresh rosemary – 3 tablespoons
- Olive oil – 2 tablespoons
- Minced garlic – 2 tablespoons
- Grated lemon zest – ½ teaspoon
- Salt – 1 teaspoon
- Black pepper – ½ teaspoon
- Lemon juice – 2 tablespoons

THE GLAZE

- Honey – 2 tablespoons

THE HEAT

- Cherry wood pellets

METHOD

1. Trim the excess fat of the chicken breast then cut it into ¼-inch slices.

2. Combine chopped fresh rosemary, minced garlic, grated lemon zest, salt, and black pepper then pour olive oil and lemon juice over the spices. Mix well.

3. Rub the chicken jerky with the spice mixture then marinate it for 6 hours.

4. Next, plug the wood pellet smoker then fill the hopper with the wood pellet. Turn the wood pellet smoker on and set the temperature to 160°F (71°C).

5. Arrange the seasoned chicken jerky in the wood pellet smoker and smoke for 6 hours.

6. Once it is done, remove from the wood pellet smoker and arrange the smoked chicken jerky on a tray.

7. Quickly baste honey over the smoked chicken jerky then serve.

8. Enjoy!

Buffalo Smoked Ground Chicken Jerky

(Cooking Time 7 Hours 10 Minutes)

Ingredients for 10 servings

- Ground chicken (5-lb., 2.3-kg.)

The Spices

- Salt – 1 teaspoon
- Black pepper – 1 teaspoon
- Garlic powder – 2 tablespoons
- Onion powder – 2 tablespoons
- Celery seed – ½ teaspoon

THE GLAZE

- Hot sauce – ½ cup

THE HEAT

- Alder wood pellets

METHOD

1. Place the ground chicken in a container then season with salt, black pepper, garlic powder, onion powder, and celery seeds. Mix well.

2. Let the seasoned chicken sit for t least 3 hours and store in the fridge to keep it fresh.

3. Next, plug the wood pellet smoker then fill the hopper with the wood pellet. Turn the wood pellet smoker on and set the temperature to 145°F (63°C).

4. Fill a jerky gun with the seasoned ground chicken then pipe on a dehydrator tray.

5. Place the tray in the wood pellet smoker and smoke the chicken jerky for 7 hours or until the chicken is no longer pink.

6. Baste hot sauce over the smoked chicken jerky and continue smoking for 30 minutes.

7. Once it is done, remove the smoked chicken jerky from the wood pellet smoker and place it on a serving dish.

8. Serve and enjoy.

CHAPTER-3 FISH

Smoked Salmon Jerky Black Pepper

(Cooking Time 7 Hours 10 Minutes)

Ingredients for 10 servings

- Salmon fillet (2-lbs., 0.9-kg.)

The Marinade

- Black pepper – 1 tablespoon

- Soy sauce – 1 cup

- Lemon juice – 2 tablespoons

- Brown sugar – 2 tablespoons

- Liquid smoke – 1 tablespoon

- Garlic powder – ½ tablespoon

- Cayenne pepper – ¼ teaspoon

- Salt – ½ teaspoon

The Heat

- Cherry wood pellets

METHOD

1. Using a sharp knife cut the salmon fillet into ½-inch sticks then place in a zipper-lock plastic bag.

2. Add black pepper, lemon juice, brown sugar, liquid smoke, garlic powder, cayenne pepper, and salt to the soy sauce then stir until mixed.

3. Pour the liquid mixture into the zipper-lock plastic bag then shake until the salmon jerky is completely coated with the spice mixture.

4. Marinate the salmon jerky for at least 6 hours or overnight and store in the fridge to keep the salmon jerky fresh.

5. Once the salmon jerky is enough marinated, remove from the fridge and thaw at room temperature.

6. Place the seasoned salmon in a colander and discard the liquid.

7. Next, plug the wood pellet smoker then fill the hopper with the wood pellet. Turn the wood pellet smoker on and set the temperature to 145°F (63°C).

8. Smoke the salmon jerky for 7 hours but check the doneness every few hours.

9. Once the smoked salmon jerky is done, remove from the wood pellet smoker and place it on a serving dish.

10. Serve and enjoy.

Sweet Lemon Smoked Trout Jerky

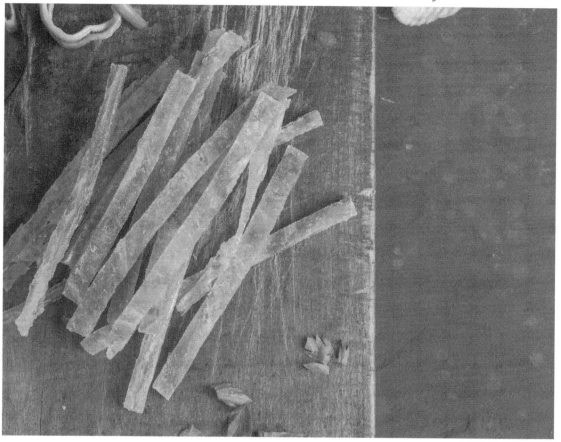

(Cooking Time 6 Hours 10 Minutes)

INGREDIENTS FOR **10** SERVINGS

- Trout fillet (2.5-lb., 2.3-kg.)

THE MARINADE

- Soy sauce – 1 cup

- Fish sauce – 1 teaspoon

- Oyster sauce – 1 teaspoon

- Molasses – 2 tablespoons

- Lemon juice – 2 tablespoons

- Black pepper – 1 teaspoon

- Liquid smoke – 1 teaspoon

- Onion powder – 2 teaspoons

THE HEAT

- Cherry wood pellets

METHOD

1. Freeze the trout fillet for 30 minutes to an hour then take it out.

2. Using a sharp knife cut the trout fillet into ½-inch sticks then set aside.

3. Combine soy sauce with the remaining marinade ingredients—fish sauce, oyster sauce, molasses, lemon juice, black pepper, liquid smoke, and onion powder. Mix well.

4. Season the trout jerky with the spice mixture then marinate for at least 6 hours or overnight.

5. Remove the marinated trout from the fridge and thaw at room temperature.

6. Arrange the seasoned trout jerky on a dehydrated tray then set aside.

7. Next, plug the wood pellet smoker then fill the hopper with the wood pellet. Turn the wood pellet smoker on and set the temperature to 145°F (63°C).

8. Place the tray with seasoned trout jerky into the wood pellet smoker then smoke the trout jerky for 6 hours.

9. Once it is done, remove the tray from the wood pellet smoker and transfer the smoked trout jerky to a serving dish.

10. Serve and enjoy.

Special Maple Smoked Salmon Jerky

(Cooking Time 6 Hours 30 Minutes)

Ingredients for 10 servings

- Salmon fillet (3-lb., 1.4-kg.)

The Marinade

- Maple syrup – 1 cup

- Grated ginger – ¼ teaspoon

- Lemon juice – 2 tablespoons

- Soy sauce – 2 tablespoons

- Black pepper – ½ teaspoon

- Salt – ¼ teaspoon

THE GLAZE

- Maple syrup – 3 tablespoons

THE HEAT

- Cherry wood pellets

METHOD

1. Cut the salmon fillet into ½-inch sticks then place in a zipper-lock plastic bag.

2. Pour the marinade ingredients mixture—maple syrup, grated ginger, lemon juice, soy sauce, black pepper, and salt into the zipper-lock plastic bag then shake to season the salmon jerky.

3. Marinate the salmon jerky for at least 6 hours or overnight and store in the fridge to keep it fresh.

4. Next, plug the wood pellet smoker then fill the hopper with the wood pellet. Turn the wood pellet smoker on and set the temperature to 145°F (63°C).

5. Directly arrange the seasoned salmon jerky on the wood pellet smoker grates then smoke for 6 hours.

6. Once it is done, baste maple syrup over the smoked salmon jerky then continue smoking for 30 minutes.

7. Remove the smoked salmon jerky from the wood pellet smoker and transfer it to a serving dish.

8. Serve and enjoy.

Superhot Smoked Tuna Jerky Tabasco

(Cooking Time 6 Hours 30 Minutes)

Ingredients for 10 servings

- Tuna fillet (2.5-lb., 2.3-kg.)

The Marinade

- Soy sauce – ¾ cup
- Molasses – 1 ½ tablespoons
- White sugar – 1 ½ tablespoons
- Worcestershire sauce – 1 ½ tablespoons
- Lemon juice – 1 ½ tablespoons
- Ground black pepper – 1 teaspoon
- Liquid smoke – 1 ½ teaspoons
- Tabasco – 1 teaspoon

THE HEAT

- Cherry wood pellets

METHOD

1. Remove the tuna skin and cut the tuna fillet into ½ inch sticks.

2. Next, pour soy sauce into a container then add molasses, white sugar, Worcestershire sauce, lemon juice, black pepper, liquid smoke, and Tabasco. Stir until combined.

3. Add the tuna sticks to the spice mixture and make sure that the tuna jerky is completely soaked into the spice mixture.

4. Marinate the tuna jerky for at least 6 hours or overnight and store in the fridge to keep it fresh.

5. Remove the tuna jerky from the fridge and thaw at room temperature.

6. After that, plug the wood pellet smoker then fill the hopper with the wood pellet. Turn the wood pellet smoker on and set the temperature to 145°F (63°C).

7. Arrange the tuna jerky in the wood pellet smoker and smoke for 6 hours or it is no longer pink. The smoked tuna jerky will crack but not break.

8. Remove the smoked tuna jerky from the wood pellet smoker and transfer it to a serving dish.

9. Serve and enjoy.

CHAPTER-4 VENISON & GAME

SMOKED VENISON JERKY IN HOT SAUCE COLA MARINADE

(COOKING TIME 6 HOURS 10 MINUTES)

Ingredients for 10 servings

- Venison (5-lb., 2.3-kg.)

The Marinade

- Soy sauce – 2 cups

- Cola – 1 ½ cups

- Worcestershire sauce – ½ cup

- Brown sugar – ¼ cup

- Hot sauce – 1 tablespoon

- Onion powder – 1 tablespoon

- Garlic powder – 1 tablespoon

- Black pepper – ½ teaspoon

- Liquid smoke – 1 teaspoon

The Heat

- Cherry and Apple wood pellets

METHOD

1. Trim the excess fat from the venison then cut into ¼-inch slices. Set aside.

2. Pour soy sauce and cola into a container then add Worcestershire sauce, brown sugar, hot sauce, onion powder, garlic powder, black pepper, and liquid smoke to the container. Stir until incorporated.

3. Season the venison jerky with the spice mixture and marinate for at least 8 hours or overnight. Store in the fridge to keep it fresh.

4. On the next day, remove the marinated venison from the fridge and thaw at room temperature.

5. Place the marinated venison jerky in a colander and discard the liquid.

6. Next, plug the wood pellet smoker then fill the hopper with the wood pellet. Turn the wood pellet smoker on and set the temperature to 185°F (85°C).

7. Using skewers prick the venison jerky and place in between the wood pellet smoker grates.

8. Smoke the venison jerky for 6 hours and once it is done, remove from the wood pellet smoker and transfer the smoked venison jerky to a serving dish.

9. Serve and enjoy.

COFFEE CHILI SMOKED VENISON JERKY

(COOKING TIME 7 HOURS 10 MINUTES)

Ingredients for 10 servings

- Venison (4-lbs., 1.8-kg.)

The Marinade

- Brewed coffee – 2 cups
- Ground coffee – 3 tablespoons
- Liquid smoke – 3 tablespoons
- Chili powder – 3 tablespoons
- Brown sugar – ¼ cup
- Smoked paprika – 3 tablespoons
- Cumin – 1 tablespoon
- Salt – 1 tablespoon

The Heat

- Mesquite wood pellets

METHOD

1. Combine brewed coffee with fresh ground coffee, liquid smoke, chili powder, brown sugar, smoked paprika, cumin, and salt. Stir until incorporated.

2. Cut the venison into ¼-inch slices then put them into the coffee mixture. Make sure that the venison jerky is completely soaked into the coffee mixture.

3. Marinate the venison jerky overnight and store it in the fridge to keep it fresh.

4. On the next day, take the marinated venison jerky out of the fridge and thaw at room temperature.

5. Transfer the marinated venison jerky to a colander and strain well.

6. Next, plug the wood pellet smoker then fill the hopper with the wood pellet. Turn the wood pellet smoker on and set the temperature to 170°F (77°C).

7. Using skewers prick the seasoned venison jerky and hang them between the wood pellet smoker grates.

8. Smoked the venison jerky for 7 hours and once it is done, remove from the wood pellet smoker and transfer to a serving dish.

9. Serve and enjoy.

Mustard Maple Marinade Smoked Sweet Venison Jerky

(Cooking Time 7 Hours 10 Minutes)

Ingredients for 10 servings

- Venison (3.5-lb., 2.3-kg.)

The Marinade

- Mustard – ¾ cup

- Maple syrup – 1 cup

- Salt – 1 teaspoon

- Liquid smoke – 1 teaspoon

- Water – ½ cup

The Heat

- Cherry wood pellets

Method

1. Combine the entire marinade ingredients—mustard, maple syrup, salt, liquid smoke, and water in a bowl then stir well. Set aside.

2. Next, cut the venison into ⅛-inch slices then place in a zipper-lock plastic bag.

3. Pour the liquid spice mixture into the plastic bag and shake until the venison jerky is coated with the seasoning mixture.

4. Marinate the venison jerky for at least 8 hours and store in the fridge to keep it fresh.

5. After 8 hours, take the marinated venison jerky out of the plastic bag and thaw at room temperature.

6. After that, plug the wood pellet smoker then fill the hopper with the wood pellet. Turn the wood pellet smoker on and set the temperature to 165°F (74°C).

7. Arrange the seasoned venison jerky directly on the wood pellet smoker grates then smoke for 7 hours.

8. Once it is done, remove the smoked jerky from the wood pellet smoker and transfer it to a serving dish.

9. Serve and enjoy.

Chewy Honey Ginger Smoked Ground Venison Jerky

(Cooking Time 10 Hours 10 Minutes)

Ingredients for 10 servings

- Ground venison (3-lb., 1.4-kg.)

The Spices

- Brown sugar – ¼ cup

- Soy sauce – 3 tablespoons

- Honey – 2 tablespoons

- Minced garlic – 2 tablespoons

- Ground ginger – ½ teaspoon

- Cornstarch – 2 tablespoons

- Worcestershire sauce – ¼ cup

- Black pepper – ½ teaspoon

The Heat

- Cherry wood pellets

METHOD

1. Season the ground venison with brown sugar, soy sauce, honey, minced garlic, ground ginger, cornstarch, Worcestershire sauce, and black pepper then mix well.

2. Fill the seasoned ground venison into a jerky gun then pipe on a dehydrator tray.

3. Next, plug the wood pellet smoker then fill the hopper with the wood pellet. Turn the wood pellet smoker on and set the temperature to 165°F (74°C).

4. Place the tray with ground venison jerky in the wood pellet smoker and smoke for 10 hours.

5. Check the smoked ground venison jerky once every few hours, and once it is done and the venison jerky is no longer pink, remove from the wood pellet smoker.

6. Arrange the smoked ground venison jerky on a serving dish and serve.

7. Enjoy!

Sweet Smoked Goose Jerky Bacon

(Cooking Time 4 Hours 10 Minutes)

INGREDIENTS FOR **10** SERVINGS

- Goose breast (3-lb., 1.4-kg.)

THE BRINE

- Water – 1 quart
- Brewed coffee – 2 cups
- Salt – 1 cup
- Brown sugar – 2 cups

THE MARINADE

- Soy sauce – ½ cup
- Brown sugar – ¾ cup
- Onion powder – 2 tablespoons
- Garlic powder – 2 tablespoons
- Sriracha sauce – 2 tablespoons

THE HEAT

- Cherry wood pellets

METHOD

1. Cut the goose breast into ¼-inch slices and set aside.

2. Pour water into a container then season with salt, brown sugar, and brewed coffee. Mix well.

3. Add the goose jerky to the brine mixture and soak overnight. Store in the fridge to keep it fresh.

4. On the next day, take the goose jerky out of the fridge then wash and rinse it. Pat the goose jerky dry.

5. Next, combine the marinade ingredients—soy sauce, brown sugar, onion powder, garlic powder, and sriracha sauce then stir until incorporated.

6. Season the goose jerky with the spice mixture and marinate for an hour.

7. After that, plug the wood pellet smoker then fill the hopper with the wood pellet. Turn the wood pellet smoker on and set the temperature to 185°F (85°C).

8. Arrange the goose jerky directly on the wood pellet smoker grates and smoke for 2 hours.

9. Flip the goose jerky and smoke for another 2 hours.

10. On the smoked goose jerky is done, remove from the wood pellet smoker and transfer to a serving dish.

11. Serve and enjoy.

Habanero Pepper Spicy Smoked Duck Jerky

(Cooking Time 4 Hours 10 Minutes)

Ingredients for 10 servings

- Duck breast (3.5-lb., 2.3-kg.)

The Marinade

- Apple cider vinegar – 2 ½ teaspoons
- Onion powder – 1 ½ teaspoons
- Garlic powder – 2 ½ teaspoons
- Salt – ¾ teaspoons
- Soy sauce – 1 cup
- Worcestershire sauce – ¾ cup
- Brown sugar – 2 tablespoons
- Black pepper – 1 teaspoon
- Smoked paprika – 2 teaspoons
- Cayenne pepper – 2 teaspoons
- Minced habanero pepper – 1 tablespoons

The Heat

- Cherry wood pellets

METHOD

1. Combine the marinade ingredients—apple cider vinegar, onion powder, garlic powder, salt, soy sauce, Worcestershire sauce, brown sugar, black pepper, smoked paprika, cayenne pepper, and minced habanero pepper in a zipper-lock plastic bag. Stir well.

2. Cut the duck breast into ¼-inch slices then place in the plastic bag. Shake and make sure that the duck jerky is completely coated with the seasoning mixture.

3. Marinate the duck jerky overnight and store it in the fridge to keep it fresh.

4. On the next day, remove the marinated duck jerky from the fridge and thaw at room temperature.

5. Plug the wood pellet smoker then fill the hopper with the wood pellet. Turn the wood pellet smoker on and set the temperature to 185°F (85°C).

6. Place the marinated duck jerky directly on the wood pellet smoker grates and smoke for 4 hours.

7. Once it is done, remove the smoked duck jerky from the wood pellet smoker and transfer it to a serving dish.

8. Serve and enjoy.

CHAPTER-5 OTHER

SMOKED EGGPLANT JERKY GARLIC

(COOKING TIME 4 HOURS 10 MINUTES)

Ingredients for 10 servings

- Eggplant (2-lbs., 0.9-kg.)

The Rub

- Smoked paprika – 1 ½ tablespoons

- Garlic powder – ¾ teaspoon

- Onion powder – ¾ teaspoon

The Heat

- Apple wood pellets

Method

1. Combine smoked paprika with garlic powder and onion powder then mix well. Set aside.

2. Cut the eggplants into ¼-inch long slices then rub with the spice mixture. Set aside.

3. Next, plug the wood pellet smoker then fill the hopper with the wood pellet. Turn the wood pellet smoker on and set the temperature to 145°F (63°C).

4. Arrange the eggplant jerky directly on the wood pellet smoker and smoke for 4 hours.

5. Once the smoked eggplant jerky is done and crispy, remove from the wood pellet smoker and transfer to a serving dish.

6. Serve and enjoy.

Spicy Cayenne Smoked Zucchini Jerky

(Cooking Time 6 Hours 10 Minutes)

INGREDIENTS FOR 10 SERVINGS

- Zucchini (3-lb., 1.3-kg.)

THE MARINADE

- Soy sauce – ¼ cup

- Maple syrup – 3 tablespoons

- Balsamic vinegar – ½ tablespoon

- Ground ginger – ½ teaspoon

- Cayenne pepper – ½ teaspoon

- Liquid smoke – 1 teaspoon

THE HEAT

- Cherry wood pellets

METHOD

1. Cut the zucchini into ¼-inch long slices then place in a zipper-lock plastic bag.

2. Next, combine soy sauce, maple syrup, balsamic vinegar, ground ginger, cayenne pepper, and liquid smoke in a bowl then stir well.

3. Pour the spice mixture into the plastic bag with zucchini jerky and shake until the zucchini jerky is completely coated with the spice mixture.

4. Marinate the zucchini jerky for an hour and set aside.

5. After an hour, plug the wood pellet smoker then fill the hopper with the wood pellet. Turn the wood pellet smoker on and set the temperature to 145°F (63°C).

6. Take the seasoned zucchini jerky out of the plastic bag and arrange on the wood pellet smoker grates.

7. Smoke the zucchini jerky for 3 hours and flip them.

8. Continue smoking the zucchini jerky for another 3 hours and once it is done and crispy, remove the smoked zucchini jerky from the wood pellet smoker.

9. Arrange the smoked zucchini jerky on a serving dish then serve.

10. Enjoy!

Tamari Ginger Smoked Sweet Potato Jerky

(Cooking Time 4 Hours 10 Minutes)

INGREDIENTS FOR 10 SERVINGS

- Sweet Potato (4-lbs., 1.8-kg.)

THE BRINE

- Salt – 1 tablespoon

- Brown sugar – 3 tablespoons

- Water – 1 quart

THE MARINADE

- Maple syrup – ½ cup

- Tamari – 2 tablespoons

- Salt – 1 teaspoon

- Garlic powder – 1 teaspoon

- Onion powder – 1 teaspoon

- Chili powder – 1 teaspoon

- Ginger – ½ teaspoon

- White pepper – ½ teaspoon

THE HEAT

- Apple wood pellets

METHOD

1. Add salt and brown sugar to a container with water then stir until incorporated.

2. Peel and cut the sweet potatoes into ⅛-inch long slices then add to the brine mixture.

3. Soak the sweet potatoes overnight and store in the fridge to keep it fresh.

4. On the next day, remove the sweet potato jerky from the fridge then wash and rinse it. Pat the sweet potato jerky dry.

5. Next, combine maple syrup with tamari, salt, garlic powder, onion powder, chili powder, ginger, and white pepper then mix well.

6. Rub the sweet potato jerky with the spice mixture then set aside.

7. After that, plug the wood pellet smoker then fill the hopper with the wood pellet. Turn the wood pellet smoker on and set the temperature to 170°F (77°C).

8. Arrange the sweet potato jerky directly on the wood pellet smoker grates and smoke for 4 hours.

9. Check the doneness of the smoked sweet potato jerky and once it is done and crispy, remove from the wood pellet smoker.

10. Transfer the smoked sweet potato jerky to a serving dish and serve.

11. Enjoy!

Sriracha Smoked Tofu Jerky with Chipotle Powder Sprinkle

(Cooking Time 6 Hours 10 Minutes)

INGREDIENTS FOR 10 SERVINGS

- Firm tofu (2.5-lb., 2.3-kg.)

THE MARINADE

- Soy sauce – ½ cup

- Liquid smoke – 2 teaspoons

- Sriracha sauce – 3 tablespoons

- Garlic powder – 1 teaspoon

THE TOPPING

- Chipotle chili powder – 2 tablespoons

THE HEAT

- Apple wood pellets

METHOD

1. Combine soy sauce with liquid smoke, Sriracha sauce, and garlic powder then mix well.

2. Cut the firm tofu into thin long slices then marinate with the Sriracha mixture for an hour.

3. Next, plug the wood pellet smoker then fill the hopper with the wood pellet. Turn the wood pellet smoker on and set the temperature to 165°F (74°C).

4. Arrange the marinated tofu jerky directly on the wood pellet smoker grates then sprinkle chipotle chili powder over the tofu jerky. Smoke for 3 hours.

5. After 3 hours, carefully flip the tofu and continue smoking for another 3 hours.

6. Once the smoked tofu jerky is done and crispy, remove from the wood pellet smoker and transfer it to a serving dish.

7. Serve and enjoy.

Smoked Bacon Jerky with Sweet Marinade

(Cooking Time 3 Hours 10 Minutes)

Ingredients for 10 servings

- Bacon (4-lbs., 1.8-kg.)

The Marinade

- Brown sugar – 1 cup
- Honey – ½ cup
- Sriracha sauce – ¼ cup
- Black pepper – ½ teaspoon

The Heat

- Cherry wood pellets

Method

1. Combine brown sugar with honey, Sriracha sauce, and black pepper then mix well.

2. Rub the bacon with the spice mixture then marinate for 30 minutes.

3. Next, plug the wood pellet smoker then fill the hopper with the wood pellet. Turn the wood pellet smoker on and set the temperature to 225°F (107°C).

4. Arrange the bacon jerky directly on the wood pellet smoker grates and smoke for an hour.

5. After an hour of smoking, flip the bacon jerky while checking the color of the smoked bacon jerky.

6. Decrease the temperature of the wood pellet smoker and continue smoking the bacon jerky for another 2 hours.

7. Once the smoked bacon jerky is done and crunchy, remove from the wood pellet smoker and transfer to a serving dish.

8. Serve and enjoy.

CHAPTER-6 WHAT IS A JERKY?

Strictly speaking, Jerky is a lean meat that has been very carefully trimmed of fat and cut up into thin bite-sized strips. The sliced portions are then further process by drying them in an oven or dehydrator. Jerkies have proven themselves to be very nutrient dense food that is lightweight and high in protein. The word "Jerky" itself is believed that have been derived from ch'arki, which is a Quechuan word that roughly translates to "dried, salted meat". In most cases, a good slab of meat can produce a large portion of Jerkys, which makes these perfect for an outdoor party snack or just a homemade snack for the lazy hours.

Just to give you a rough idea, the 16-ounce meat will yield approximately 4 ounces of freshly prepared dried jerky.It is understandable that a dehydrator might not be available in every homestead; however having an oven is pretty common. To make sure that maximum people are able to experience the joy of preparing jerky using my book, all of the recipes in this book only require an oven to prepare them properly. It should also be noted that in some countries, Jerkys are actually prepared by drying the meat under the sun! However, it is strictly advised to refrain from such practice. While previously Jerky's were made only using some salt and drying them, modern-day Jerky tend to exhibit a lot of flavors thank their amazing marinades as you will see throughout the book. For one the temperature outside will constantly keep fluctuating and secondly, it won't kill off the harmful pathogens present in the meat, which might lead to serious illness.

That being said, the process of properly ensuring full safety measures for jerky can be divided into 2 parts.

- Environmental sanitation
- Killing off the meat pathogens

It is of utmost importance that the place where you are going to cut and process the meat is in tip-top condition to ensure that no contamination takes place prior to drying the jerky.

CHOOSING YOUR MEAT

When it comes to choosing your meat, the following guidelines should help you.

BEEF: Try to always go for lean cuts, preferably chuck, round, flank, sirloin and rump.

GAME MEATS: For game meats, most preferred ones include Venison, antelope, elk, and Deer. Best cuts include loin, flank and round. Try to avoid cougar, bear and feral hog though as they might contain Trichinella parasites.

POULTRY AND RABBIT: For such meats, best cuts are breast, leg, and thigh. Loin also works, particularly in case of rabbits.

FISH: Go for fish that are non-oily as the high-fat content of those fish might lead to early spoilage. Salmon, Tuna, Trout are good options.

GROUND MEAT: For using ground meat for jerky, make sure to go for meat that is at least 93% lean.

CHAPTER-7 SAFETY FIRST!

Preparing homemade Jerky isn't really that much difficult at all. However, the main concern comes from the fact that raw meats tend to have the risk of spreading diseases and pathogens including that of Salmonella and E. coli. However, it should be noted that for an individual to actually become infected by such diseases through Jerky eating, the following chain of events needs to take place.

- The meat that is being used must be contaminated with a pathogenic organism
- The pathogen must survive the process of making the jerky
- The individual must consume the jerky

The good news is that, through some proper maintenance and safety regulations, such risk can be easily avoided altogether. In fact, when preparing properly, most if not all of the harmful pathogens present in meat are completely destroyed. Now, you might be wondering if the traditional process of simply drying the jerky would kill off the pathogens. Unfortunately, the answer to that question is a big "No". Simply drying the jerky at 140-155 degree Fahrenheit/60-68 degree Celsius does not fully make the Jerky safe to eat. As mentioned earlier, there are specific steps of sanitizing the jerky, which you should go through. In this chapter, I will be discussing the various safety precautions, which you should follow in order to ensure that your jerky is clean and pristine from the inside and out.

A universally accepted method of ensuring this is to follow the standard rule of the 4 C's, which includes:

- Keeping your meat **CLEAN**
- Keeping your meat **COLD**
- Keeping your meat **COVERED**
- And keeping your meat free from **CROSS-CONTAMINATION**

Cleanliness of the meat

If you can make sure to follow the steps below, you will be able to ensure that your meat is safe from any kind of bacterial or airborne contamination. This first step is very much essential as no market bought or freshly cut meat is completely sterile.

Following these, would greatly minimize the risk of getting affected by diseases.

- Make sure to properly wash your hands before beginning to process your meat. Use fresh tap water and soap/hand sanitizer.
- Make sure to remove any metal ornaments such as rings and watches from your wrist and hand before starting to handle the meat.
- Thoroughly clean the cutting surface using sanitizing liquid to remove any grease or unwanted contaminants. If you want to go for a homemade sanitizer, then you can simply make a solution of 1 part chlorine bleach and 10 parts water.
- The above-mentioned sanitizer should also be used to soak your tools such as knives and other equipment to ensure that they are safe to use as well.
- Alternatively, commercial acid based/ no rinsed sanitizer such as Star San will also work.
- After each and every use, all of the knives and other equipment such as meat grinders, slicers, extruders etc. should be cleaned thoroughly using soap water. The knives should be taken care in particular by cleaning the place just on top of the handle as it might contain blood and pieces of meat.
- When it comes to cleaning the surface, you should use cloths or sponges.

A NOTE OF SPONGES/CLOTHES:

It is ideal that you keep your sponge or cleaning cloth clean as it might result in cross-contamination. These are an ideal harboring place for foodborne pathogens. Just follow the simple steps to ensure that you are on the safe side:

- Make sure to clean your sponge daily. It is seen that the effectiveness of cleaning it increases if you microwave dam sponge for 1 minute and disinfect it using a solution of ¼ -1/2 teaspoon of concentrated bleach. This process will kill 99% of bacteria.

- Replace your sponge frequently as using the same sponge every single time (even with wash) will result in eventual bacterial growth.

- When not using the sponge, keep it in a dry place, making sure to wring it off of any loose food or debris.

KEEPING YOUR MEAT COLD

Mismanagement of temperature is one of the most common reasons for outbreaks of foodborne diseases. The study has shown that bacteria grow best at temperatures of 40 to 140 degree Fahrenheit/4-60 degree Celsius, which means that if not taken care properly, bacteria in the meat will start to multiply very quickly. The best way to prevent this from happening is to keep your meat cold before using it. Keep them eat in your fridge before processing them and make sure that the temperature is below 40 degrees Fahrenheit/4 degree Celsius.

KEEPING YOUR MEAT COVERED

All foods tend to start to diminish once they are opened from their packaging or exposed to air. However, the effect can be greatly minimized if you are able to cover or wrap the foods properly.
Same goes for meat.
Good ways of keeping your meat covered and wrapped include:

- Using aluminum foil to cover up your meat will help to protect it from light and oxygen and keep the moisture intact. However, since Aluminum is reactive, it is advised that a layer of plastic wrap is used underneath the aluminum foil to provide double protective layer.
- If keeping the meat in a bowl with no lid, then a plastic wrap can be used to seal the bowl providing an airtight enclosure.
- Re-sealable bags provide protection by storing it in a bag and squeezing out any air.
- Airtight glass or plastic containers with lids are good options as well.
- A type of paper known as Freezer paper is specifically designed to wrap foods that are to be kept in the fridge. These wraps are amazing for meat as well.
- Vacuum sealers are often used for Sous Vide packaging. These machines are a bit expensive but are able to provide excellent packaging by completely sucking out any air from a re-sealable bag. This greatly increases the meats shelf life both outside and in the fridge.

PREVENTING FORMS OF CROSS-CONTAMINATION

Cross-Contamination usually occurs when one food comes into contact with another. In our case, we are talking about our meats.

This can be avoided very easily by keeping the following things in check:

- Always wash your hands thoroughly with warm water. Also, the cutting boards, counters, knives and other utensils should also be cleaned as instructed at the first section of the chapter.
- Make sure to keep different types of meat in different bowls, dishes, and plates prior to using them.
- When storing the meat in the fridge, make sure to keep the raw meat, seafood, poultry and eggs on the bottom shelf of your fridge and in individual sealed containers.
- Keep your refrigerator shelves cleaned and juices from meat/vegetables might drip on them.
- Always refrain yourself from keeping raw meat/vegetables on the same plate as cooked goods.
- Always make sure to clean your cutting boards and use different cutting boards for different types of foods. Raw meats, vegetables, and other foods should not be cut using the same table.

Clearing out the pathogens from your Jerky

As mentioned earlier, simply drying the jerky at 155 degrees Fahrenheit/68 degree Celsius won't completely kill the pathogens from your meat. Therefore it is essential pre-kill the pathogens from your jerky before drying it.

The following three methods have been proven to kill most of the pathogens with ease. You may use whichever you want.

Post-Drying/Heating In Oven:

This is perhaps the easiest one of the three and produces a very traditional jerky. Once you have seasoned and fully prepared your meat, follow the steps:

- Preheat your oven to a temperature of 275 degrees Fahrenheit/135 degree Celsius
- Add the prepared jerky meat to a baking sheet, making sure that the meat is not overlapping.
- Slip the baking sheet into your oven and let them sit for 10 minutes.

Dipping your meat in the boiling marinade:

Following this process will shorten the drying time and will make your jerky tender, just do the steps below:

- Take 1-2 cups of your marinade in a saucepan and boil the mixture over medium heat
- Add the meat strips and reheat the mixture to a simmer
- Make sure to keep stirring them and simmer for about 2 minutes
- Use tongs to remove them and dry them as instructed

BAKING THE MEAT PRIOR DRYING:

This is another well-known method that has been seen to produce good results.

- Preheat your oven to 325 degrees Fahrenheit/162 degree Celsius
- Add the seasoned raw meat strips on a baking sheet and heat them up to a temperature of 160 degrees Fahrenheit/70 degree Celsius (check using an internal thermometer)
- Once the desired temperature is reached, immediately begin the drying process
- Keep in mind that the for fish, you are to increase the internal temperature to 160 degrees Fahrenheit/71 degree Celsius and hold the temperature for at least 90 seconds prior to drying

CHAPTER-8 PREPARING THE MEAT

The final step before drying the meat is to prepare the meat themselves. Keep in mind that procedures here are detailed out very elaborately while they are written in the recipes briefly. If you ever find yourself to be confused, just simply go through this chapter to clarify your confusion. There are two types of preparation method that you should keep in mind.

- For ground meat
- For slicing whole meat

CUTTING THE WHOLE JERKY

- The first step is to choose your lean meat (Instructions given in the first chapter)
- Let the meat chill in your fridge until it has a temperature below 30-40 degree Fahrenheit/-1 to 4 degree Celsius. This will make the meat firm and it will make it easier for you to cut it
- Slice off the surface fat as much as you can
- Trim off the silver skin and discard it
- Once you are done, the meat is then ready to be sliced up
- For slicing the meat, wear a mesh glove as protection and slowly apply pressure on your knife
- Cut it against the grain into comfortable ¼ inch thick strips
- While cutting the meat, try to keep a bowl of water nearby for dipping your knife periodically

Preparing ground meat

The process of preparing ground meat is slightly different than that of the whole meat, but not difficult at all!

Just follow the process below:

1. Thoroughly wash your hand and cutting surface
2. Cut your meat into small chunks suitable for your meat grinder
3. Season the small portions with seasoning
4. Grind the seasoned chunks carefully
5. Allow the ground meat to fall into a clean container
6. Use a clean meat stomper to carefully push away any wayward chunks into the grinders throat
7. Put the ground meat into your fridge and allow it to chill
8. Clean the grinder
9. Move on to shaping the meat

N.B: Keep in mind that if you have purchased already ground meat, then you should skip steps 1-7 and 8 and directly move to shaping the meat.

Shaping your meat

Shaping the meat won't be required for whole meat slices; however, the shaping is much more required when it comes to dealing with ground meat. Ground meat can be formed into either strip or can be fashioned into small pieces or nuggets.

Make sure to thoroughly wash your hand and wear rubber gloves.

- Mix the cure, flavoring, and seasoning according to your recipes
- Begin forming the meat into strips by placing them on a sheet of freezer paper or wax paper
- Place the second sheet of wax/freezer paper on top and use a rolling pin to roll out the meat to ¼ inch thick patty
- Peel off the upper paper and use a clean knife and slice the flat meat into 1 inch wide strips
- Make sure to avoid tearing the strips apart while transferring them to jerky wrack
- Once you have transferred them, flip the wax/freezer paper onto your rack and peel it off, which should leave the strips
- Dry them accordingly

A NOTE ON CURING MEAT

The art of curing meat has been around since the ancient days! Simply put, this is a process through which meats are preserved for a really long time without the use of any harmful chemicals.

All you need for the process are salt, nitrites and most importantly, a lot of time! Over time, the meat that you are processing will turn from a water packed and pliable piece to a stiff and dry meat with deliciously infused flavors. Generally speaking, dry cured meat is often said to pack a very soul touching Umami-flavor that tends to be both enlightening and mouthwatering. Interested to know the process? Well, the basic procedure of curing meat goes as follows!

STEP 1: Decide the meat that you are going to cure. Most preferred parts include Pork loin and belly, brisket, beef hindquarter, mutton legs and duck breast.

STEP 2: Trim off any excess fat, meat or tendons that might be hanging from your meat.

STEP 3: If you have large sized meat, then try using a prong and stabbing it to ensure that you get better salt coverage. Make sure to do this just before applying your rub.

STEP 4: Decide the kind of cure that you are going to use (the rub) and prepare the mixture accordingly.

STEP 5: A general cure mixture would have a ratio of 2:1000 sodium nitrate and salt. This essentially means that you are to add 1000g of salt for every 2 grams of sodium nitrite. Make the mixture accordingly.

STEP 6: Add any spices to the curing mixture if required. Some include:
- Peppercorns
- Sugar
- Coriander
- Star Anise
- Fennel Seed
- Citrus Zest

STEP 7: Rub the mixture all over your meat using your hand. Make sure that the whole meat is covered properly.
As a precaution, make sure to not use metal trays (or even if you do use metal trays, use parchment paper).

STEP 8: Allow the meat to refrigerate in your fridge for about 7-10 days depending on the size of your meat. Keep a small part of the meat uncovered to allow for proper air flow.

STEP 9: Remove the meat from the fridge and wash it under cold water to ensure that you are able to remove as much of the rub as possible.

STEP 10: Roll up the meat and tightly wrap it up in cheesecloth!

STEP 11: Your cured meat is ready! Label it and hang it in a cool and dark place. It can be kept for about 2 weeks to 2 months. A cool walk-in refrigerator is ideal, which provides temperatures of 70 degrees Fahrenheit/21 degree Celsius

STEP 12: Serve by removing cheesecloth and slicing it up.

CHAPTER-9 INFORMATION ON SMOKING MEAT

BARBECUING AND SMOKING MEAT

You might not believe it, but there are still people who think that the process of Barbequing and Smoking are the same! So, this is something which you should know about before diving in deeper.

So, whenever you are going to use a traditional BBQ grill, you always put your meat directly on top of the heat source for a brief amount of time which eventually cooks up the meal. Smoking, on the other hand, will

 require you to combine the heat from your grill as well as the smoke to infuse a delicious smoky texture and flavor to your meat. Smoking usually takes much longer than traditional barbecuing. In most cases, it takes a minimum of 2 hours and a temperature of 100 -120 degrees for the smoke to be properly infused into the meat. Keep in mind that the time and temperature will obviously depend on the type of meat that you are using, and that is why it is suggested that you keep a meat thermometer handy to ensure that your meat is doing fine. Keep in mind that this method of barbecuing is also known as "Low and slow" smoking as well. With that cleared up, you should be aware that there are actually two different ways through which smoking is done.

110

COLD AND HOT SMOKING

Depending on the type of grill that you are using, you might be able to get the option to go for a Hot Smoking Method or a Cold Smoking One. The primary fact about these three different cooking techniques which you should keep in mind are as follows:

- **HOT SMOKING:** In this technique, the food will use both the heat on your grill and the smoke to prepare your food. This method is most suitable for items such as chicken, lamb, brisket etc.

- **COLD SMOKING:** In this method, you are going to smoke your meat at a very low temperature such as 85 F (30 degrees Celsius), making sure that it doesn't come into the direct contact with the heat. This is mostly used as a means to preserve meat and extend their life on the shelf.

- **ROASTING SMOKE:** This is also known as Smoke Baking. This process is essentially a combined form of both roasting and baking and can be performed in any type of smoker with a capacity of reaching temperatures above 180 F (80 degrees Celsius).

SELECTING A SMOKER

You need to invest in a good smoker if you are going to smoke meat on a regular basis. Consider these options when buying a smoker. Here are two natural fire option for you:

- **CHARCOAL SMOKERS**: are fueled by a combination of charcoal and wood. Charcoal burns easily and the temperature remains steady, so you won't have any problem with a charcoal smoker. The wood gives a great flavor to the meat and you will enjoy smoking meats.

- **WOOD SMOKER:** The wood smoker will give your brisket and ribs the best smoky flavor and taste, but it is a bit harder to cook with wood. Both hardwood blocks and chips are used as fuel.

DIFFERENT SMOKER TYPES

Essentially, what you should know is that right now in the market, you are going to get three different types of Smokers.

CHARCOAL SMOKER

 These types of smokers are hands down the best one for infusing the perfect Smoky flavor to your meat. But be warned, though, that these smokers are a little bit difficult to master as the method of regulating temperature is a little bit difficult when compared to normal Gas or Electric smokers.

ELECTRIC SMOKER

After the charcoal smoker, next comes perhaps the simpler option, Electric Smokers. These are easy to use and plug and play type. All you need to do is just plug in, set the temperature and go about your daily life. The smoker will do the rest. However, keep in mind that the finishing smoky flavor won't be as intense as the Charcoal one.

GAS SMOKERS

Finally, comes the Gas Smokers. These have a fairly easy mechanism for temperature control and are powered usually by LP Gas. The drawback of these Smokers is that you are going to have to keep checking up on your Smoker every now and then to ensure that it has not run out of Gas.

DIFFERENT SMOKER STYLES

The different styles of Smokers are essentially divided into the following.

VERTICAL (BULLET STYLE USING CHARCOAL)

These are usually low-cost solutions and are perfect for first-time smokers.

VERTICAL (CABINET STYLE)

These Smokers come with a square shaped design with cabinets and drawers/trays for easy accessibility. These cookers also come with a water tray and a designated wood chips box as well.

OFFSET

These type of smokers have dedicated fireboxes that are attached to the side of the main grill. The smoke and heat required for these are generated from the firebox itself which is then passed through the main chamber and out through a nicely placed chimney.

KAMADO JOE

And finally, we have the Kamado Joe which is ceramic smokers are largely regarded as being the "Jack of All Trades".

These smokers can be used as low and slow smokers, grills, hi or low-temperature ovens and so on.

They have a very thick ceramic wall which allows it to hold heat better than any other type of smoker out there, requiring only a little amount of charcoal.

These are easy to use with better insulation and are more efficient when it comes to fuel control.

CHOOSE YOUR WOOD

You need to choose your wood carefully because the type of wood you will use affect greatly to the flavor and taste of the meat. Here are a few options for you:

- **MAPLE**: Maple has a smoky and sweet taste and goes well with pork or poultry

- **ALDER**: Alder is sweet and light. Perfect for poultry and fish.

- **APPLE**: Apple has a mild and sweet flavor. Goes well with pork, fish, and poultry.

- **OAK**: Oak is great for slow cooking. Ideal for game, pork, beef, and lamb.

- **MESQUITE**: Mesquite has a smoky flavor and extremely strong. Goes well with pork or beef.

- **HICKORY**: Has a smoky and strong flavor. Goes well with beef and lamb.

- **CHERRY:** Has a mild and sweet flavor. Great for pork, beef, and turkey

The Different Types Of Wood	Suitable For
Hickory	Wild game, chicken, pork, cheeses, beef
Pecan	Chicken, pork, lamb, cheeses, fish.
Mesquite	Beef and vegetables
Alder	Swordfish, Salmon, Sturgeon and other types of fishes. Works well with pork and chicken too.
Oak	Beef or briskets
Maple	Vegetable, ham or poultry
Cherry	Game birds, poultry or pork
Apple	Game birds, poultry, beef
Peach	Game birds, poultry or pork
Grape Vines	Beef, chicken or turkey
Wine Barrel Chips	Turkey, beef, chicken or cheeses
Seaweed	Lobster, mussels, crab, shrimp etc.
Herbs or Spices such as rosemary, bay leaves, mint, lemon peels, whole nutmeg etc.	Good for cheeses or vegetables and a small collection of light meats such as fillets or fish steaks.

CHARCOAL

In General, there are essentially three different types of Charcoal. All of them are basically porous residues of black color that are made of carbon and ashes. However, the following are a little bit distinguishable due to their specific features.

- **BBQ BRIQUETTES**: These are the ones that are made from a fine blend of charcoal and char.

- **CHARCOAL BRIQUETTES:** These are created by compressing charcoal and are made from sawdust or wood products.

- **LUMP CHARCOAL:** These are made directly from hardwood and are the most premium quality charcoals available. They are completely natural and are free from any form of the additive.

RIGHT TEMPERATURE

- Start at 250F (120C): Start your smoker a bit hot. This extra heat gets the smoking process going.

- Temperature drop: Once you add the meat to the smoker, the temperature will drop, which is fine.

- Maintain the temperature. Monitor and maintain the temperature. Keep the temperature steady during the smoking process.

Avoid peeking every now and then. Smoke and heat two most important element make your meat taste great. If you open the cover every now and then you lose both of them and your meat loses flavor. Only the lid only when you truly need it.

BASIC PREPARATIONS

- Always be prepared to spend the whole day and take as much time as possible to smoke your meat for maximum effect.
- Make sure to obtain the perfect Ribs/Meat for the meal which you are trying to smoke. Do a little bit of research if you need.
- I have already added a list of woods in this book, consult to that list and choose the perfect wood for your meal.
- Make sure to prepare the marinade for each of the meals properly. A great deal of the flavor comes from the rubbing.
- Keep a meat thermometer handy to get the internal temperature when needed.
- Use mittens or tongs to keep yourself safe
- Refrain yourself from using charcoal infused alongside starter fluid as it might bring a very unpleasant odor to your food
- Always make sure to start off with a small amount of wood and keep adding them as you cook.
- Don't be afraid to experiment with different types of wood for newer flavor and experiences.
- Always keep a notebook near you and note jot down whatever you are doing or learning and use them during the future session. This will help you to evolve and move forward.

-

ELEMENTS OF SMOKING

Smoking is a very indirect method of cooking that relies on a number of different factors to give you the most perfectly cooked meal that you are looking for. Each of these components is very important to the whole process as they all work together to create the meal of your dreams.

- **TIME:** Unlike grilling or even Barbequing, smoking takes a really long time and requires a whole lot of patience. It takes time for the smoky flavor to slowly get infused into the meats. Jus to bring things into comparison, it takes an about 8 minutes to fully cook a steak through direct heating, while smoking (indirect heating) will take around 35-40 minutes.

- **TEMPERATURE:** When it comes to smoking, the temperature is affected by a lot of different factors that are not only limited to the wind, cold air temperatures but also the cooking wood's dryness. Some smokers work best with large fires that are controlled by the draw of a chimney and restricted airflow through the various vents of the cooking chamber and firebox. While other smokers tend to require smaller fire with fewer coals as well as a completely different combination of the vent and draw controls. However, most smokers are designed to work at temperatures as low as 180 degrees Fahrenheit to as high as 300 degrees Fhrenheit. But the recommend temperature usually falls between 250 degrees Fahrenheit and 275 degrees Fahrenheit.

- **AIRFLOW:** The level of air to which the fire is exposed to greatly determines how your fire will burn and how quickly it will burn the fuel. For instance, if you restrict air flow into the firebox by closing up the available vents, then the fire will burn at a low temperature and vice versa. Typically in smokers, after lighting up the fire, the vents are opened to allow for maximum airflow and is then adjusted throughout the cooking process to make sure that optimum flame is achieved.

- **INSULATION:** Insulation is also very important when it comes to smokers as it helps to easily manage the cooking process throughout the whole cooking session. Good insulation allows smokers to efficiently reach the desired temperature instead of waiting for hours upon hours!

CONCLUSION

I can't express how honored I am to think that you found my book interesting and informative enough to read it all through to the end. I thank you again for purchasing this book and I hope that you had as much fun reading it as I had writing it. I bid you farewell and encourage you to move forward and find your true Smoked Meat spirit!

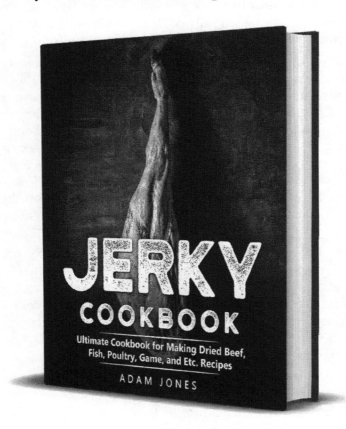

OTHER BOOKS BY ADAM JONES

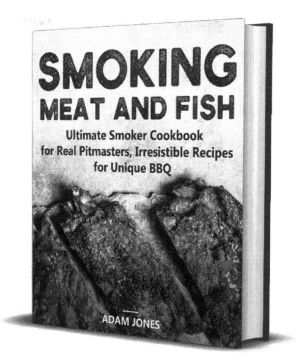

https://www.amazon.com/dp/B08B39QL1J

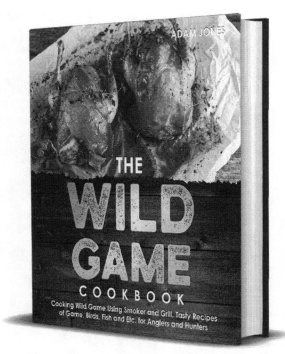

https://www.amazon.com/dp/B095BVWK21

https://www.amazon.com/dp/B08L54RVHH

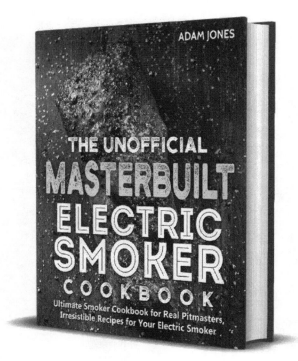

https://www.amazon.com/dp/1098708040

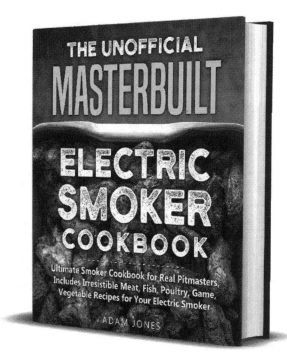

https://www.amazon.com/dp/B09L4HRD2K

https://www.amazon.com/dp/B09JKL59ML

JERKY COOKBOOK

Ultimate Cookbook for Making Dried Beef, Fish, Poultry, Game, and Etc. Recipes

ADAM JONES

Made in the USA
Las Vegas, NV
06 November 2023

80363576R00072